P&O CRUISE SHIPS

Ian Collard

AMBERLEY

First published 2017

Amberley Publishing
The Hill, Stroud, Gloucestershire, GL5 4EP
www.amberley-books.com

Copyright © Ian Collard, 2017

The right of Ian Collard to be identified as the
Author of this work has been asserted in accordance with
the Copyrights, Designs and Patents Act 1988.

ISBN 978 1 4456 6740 9 (print)
ISBN 978 1 4456 6741 6 (ebook)

British Library Cataloguing in Publication Data.
A catalogue record for this book is available from the
British Library.

Typesetting by Amberley Publishing.
Printed in Great Britain.

Introduction

In 1815 Brodie McGhie Willcox established a shipbroking company in Lime Street, London, and he appointed the Scotsman Arthur Anderson as his clerk. Anderson was born on 19 February 1792, near Lerwick in the Shetland Islands. Having volunteered for the Royal Navy at the age of sixteen, he learned his shipping business the hard way: as a captain's clerk at sea. After visiting Spain and Portugal on a regular basis, he was soon able to read and write in Spanish. Willcox was born on Ostend, Belgium, and was educated in Newcastle upon Tyne. The firm operated as voyage brokers and commission agents developing the trade to the Iberian Peninsula for seven years. The men became partners in 1822 when the company name was changed to Willcox and Anderson, operating as agents of several small sailing vessels to Spain and Portugal. The trade to Portugal involved carrying guns for the Portuguese royal family, with Anderson travelling on the first voyage to ensure delivery and payment. The rebellion collapsed and by 1833 the trade had resumed, with the company having the rights to fly the Portuguese and later the Spanish Royal Standards. The origins of P&O's house flag dates back to this period, as it contains the red and yellow of Spain and the blue and white of Portugal.

Willcox and Anderson chartered the Bourne steamers *William Fawcett* and *Royal Tar*. The Spanish Court approved a regular service by the Dublin & London Steam Packet Co. with Willcox and Anderson operating the service under the name of the Peninsular Steam Navigation Co. As the original vessels proved too small, the company chartered the *City of Londonderry* and *Liverpool*. Iberia was delivered in 1836 and weekly sailings were introduced on 1 September 1836, following the award of the mail contract. These sailings operated from London and Falmouth to Vigo, Oporto, Lisbon, Cadiz and Gibraltar, with an additional monthly service to Malta, Corfu, and Alexandria, and the opportunity to ship cargo from there to India. The company also inaugurated a service from Liverpool under the name of the Liverpool Branch Line, with vessels chartered from the Dublin & London Steam Packet Co. Ltd. *Manchester* and *City of Londonderry* were used on this route. Captain Bourne was invited to join the board of Willcox and Anderson and on 1 February 1841 the *Braganza*, *Liverpool*, *Royal Tar* and *Tagus* were purchased by the company.

In 1839 Lord William Bentinck, the Governor General of India, was dissatisfied with the arrangements for the mail contract to the subcontinent, and this was put out to tender. Willcox and Anderson secured the contract with a bid of £34,200 and *India* was built for the Indian trade. On 23 April 1840 the Board of the Peninsular Steam Navigation changed the name of the company to the Peninsular and Oriental Steam Navigation Co. Ltd. It had a share capital of £1,000,000 and became known as the P&O Line. The contract was divided into two halves – the west of Egypt and east of Egypt – and two new ships were ordered for the Suez–Bombay route – passengers would disembark at Alexandria and travel by land the 250 miles to Suez. The auxiliary branch of P&O, which was known as the Egyptian Oriental Transit Co., took over rest houses on the route and carried out various improvements, which made the lot of the traveller much better. At this time the company were stating in their announcements that two of the ships on the service to Gibraltar, the *Don Juan* and *Tagus*, were 'the largest and most powerful that have been yet put afloat'.

In 1840 P&O's chairman was the financier Sir John Larpent, while Brodie Willcox, Arthur Anderson and Francis Carleton were managing directors. A new contract was awarded by the British government for the route from Suez to Ceylon, Madras and Calcutta and from Ceylon to Penang, Singapore and Hong Kong. *Lady Mary Wood* was sent out to be the first on this service and reached Singapore on 4 August 1845, with mails forty-one days out of London, and eight days from Ceylon. On 24 September 1842 *Hindustan* sailed from Southampton to Gibraltar, St Vincent, Ascension, Cape Town, Mauritius, Port de Galle and Calcutta and took ninety-one days, of which twenty-eight were spent in port. Colliers had been sent to each port so that the ship was sure of fuel. Singapore was established as the transhipment port for the company, with Canton offering a feeder service to and from Hong Kong to Macao in 1848. The following year a service was offered between Hong Kong and Shanghai by the *Lady Mary Wood*. A parliamentary committee recommended a Singapore–Australia service and P&O's tender for this route was accepted on 26 February 1852 at a cost of £119,600 per annum. A route from Singapore to King George's Sound, Adelaide, Melbourne and Sydney was proposed.

Chusan left Southampton on 15 May 1852 for Adelaide, Melbourne and Sydney, where she arrived on 3 August. She was followed by the *Formosa*, which from then on ran from Singapore to Australia and connected at Singapore with liners from England. Later in the year *Formosa* was taken off and put on the Calcutta–China service, and her place was taken by the *Shanghai*. The Australian service soon became popular and the larger *Bombay and Madras* replaced *Chusan* later that year. However, the increase in the price of coal and P&O's commitment to mail contracts meant that they were unable to reduce the number of sailings and faced severe financial restraints. However, coal fields were discovered at Labuan and Formosa, and P&O operated the colliers *Rajah* and *Manila* to their Far East coaling station. The price of coal increased again following the outbreak of the Crimean War. The company paid no dividend in 1854 for the first time. Following the end of the war in 1856 the contract for the Australian trade was awarded to the European & Columbian Steam Navigation Co. and P&O's *Simla* was chartered to take the first sailing. A two-year contract was awarded to P&O to operate a mail service between Hong Kong and Manilla.

In 1858 the company obtained the new Australian mail contract for £118,000, which specified a passage time to Sydney of fifty-five days. The following year P&O had thoughts of providing links with Japan, and the general administration manager Thomas Sutherland visited the country. It is thought that the intense humidity of the Red Sea voyage led to the word 'posh' (port out starboard home) being used in relation to the sea journey. The cabins away from the sun were the coolest; outward these were on the port or left, while homeward they were on the opposite or starboard side. Consequently, regular travellers would book a cabin port out starboard home, which was later abbreviated to POSH. P&O were becoming a household name and its fleet was multiplying to keep pace with its ever-increasing service commitments. In 1859 the fleet consisted of fifty-five liners, of which thirty-eight were screw steamers.

Mooltan was completed in 1861 and she was their first steamer to have compound engines, or inverted tandem compound engines. This machinery offered considerable economy in fuel consumption, and she was notable as having a hydraulic machine for making ice for the passengers. By now ships were being added to the fleet nearly every year. The 1860s marked the period of change to screw propulsion from paddles. In the early years of the company paddles had been the only method of propulsion, and the first screw steamer was the *Benares* in 1858. From then on the change to screw was not even gradual. In 1858 three other screw steamers were added in addition to the *Benares*, and in 1859 two more were added – the *Napaul* and *Jeddo*. Between 1861 and 1864 eight screw steamers were added, and only two paddlers, one of which, the *Nyanza* in 1864, was P&O's last vessel to be so propelled.

Brodie Willcox died in 1862 and a new mail contract was signed two years later, with P&O being the sole tenderers. Arthur Anderson died in 1868 and Thomas Sutherland was appointed an assistant manager. The Suez Canal was opened on 17 November 1869 with the P&O vessel *Delta* carrying the official guests in a procession of sixty-eight ships. The canal changed the nature of travel in the area, making most of P&O's investments redundant. Prior to the opening of the canal the company owned wharfs, tugs and barges and had maintained supply stores, farms, a water distillery and an ice-making plant. Freight rates were reduced, making some ships uneconomical to operate. The big fleets suitable for European trade at one end and Eastern trade at the other had to be replaced by ships designed for through traffic. Thomas Sutherland was appointed managing director in 1872. Sutherland authorised the building of new ships, with eleven vessels delivered in 1873. The following year the mail contracts were renegotiated, with the land transhipment clause being deleted; however, the subsidy was reduced by £20,000. The head office was transferred from Southampton to London. Between 1870 and 1880 thirty vessels joined the fleet, all with inverted compound engines. Then there was the odd tandem compound machine and, in the course of time, the triple expansion engine came into its own.

At least three-quarters of Australia's total overseas trade in the nineteenth century was with England, but in the 1880s foreign buyers began to take a closer interest in the Australian wool auctions. Direct commerce with the European mainland started in 1883, when Messageries Maritimes began their Australian service. Four years later Norddeutscher Lloyd began shipping Australian wool to German, Dutch and Belgian ports. The volume of shipping engaged in the Australian trade was 16 million tons in 1861, and this rose steadily towards the end of the century. The wheat, meat and dairy industries continued to expand in the 1880s, and more ships were needed to carry their produce to Europe.

Sutherland became chairman in 1881 and, following unrest at Alexandria the following year, it was decided that all mail should go by ship through the Suez Canal. *Victoria*, *Britannia*, *Arcadia* and *Oceana* were built to celebrate the twin Golden Jubilees of Queen Victoria and P&O. They were known as the Jubilee Class, with gross registers of over 6,000 tons and lengths of over 460 feet. A service to Australia via the Cape was introduced in 1889 but this proved unsuccessful due to pressure from the established Union and Castle companies. However, the Blue Anchor Line operated emigrant steamers to Australia via the Cape and the fleet and goodwill of this company was acquired in 1910 for £275,000. P&O soon established that the Blue Anchor ships *Commonwealth*, *Narrung*, *Wakool*, *Wilcannia* and *Geelong* were not suitable, and the first of the 'B' class of 1911 and 1912, *Ballarat*, *Beltana*, *Benalla*, *Berrima* and *Borda*, were delivered. They were over 11,000 tons, and had large cargo capacity as well as insulated stowage for meat, and carried around 1,100 single-class passengers. The service was named the P&O Branch Line and it was specified by South Africa that the ships carry all-white crews. Between 1900 and 1902 during the Boer War, nine P&O vessels were employed as troopships, transporting over 150,000 service personnel. *Marmora*, completed in 1903, was the company's first vessel of over 10,000 tons and she was eclipsed before the outbreak of the First World War by ships of 12,400 tons, such as the *Medina* and *Maloja* of 1911.

In 1914 the Australian United Steam Navigation Co. was acquired and an amalgamation was made between P&O and the British India Line, where there was the exchange by each company of £7,000,000 of preference stock, and P&O transferred £638,123 of deferred stock for 1 million British India shares. The joint board of directors comprised twelve P&O members and eight from the British India Company. There was a fusion of the business by the interchange of stock. British India's routes were complementary to P&O and it owned 131 vessels, with a gross tonnage of 598,203. On the outbreak of the First World War, *Mantua* was cruising in the Baltic and she was instructed to return to the United Kingdom immediately. Furniture and fittings were used as fuel to ensure that she returned home without incident. She was soon converted as the first P&O armed merchant cruiser, together with *Macedonia*. *Himalaya* was at Penang and she was ordered to sail to Hong Kong, where she was fitted with eight 4.7-inch guns. Forty-four ships, with a combined tonnage of 284,716, were lost in 1917, and fourteen were lost the following year.

On 1 July 1916 P&O acquired the New Zealand Shipping Co. and the Federal Steam Navigation Co. with a mutual exchange of shares. The London shipbroking firm of Birt, Potter & Hughes also joined the P&O group of companies. The majority of ordinary shares of the Union Steamship Co. of New Zealand were acquired in August the following year, with Hain and Norse Lines becoming part of the group. At the end of the First World War the company owned forty-four vessels and had lost nineteen ships during hostilities. The Khedivial Mail Line was acquired in 1919 but was never profitable because of the unstable political situation in the Middle East, and Lord Inchcape negotiated its sale in 1924. Losses in the war and the fact that new ships could not be built left the company with areas to make up after hostilities ceased. Initially they bought some standard ships on the stocks for conversion and acquired some ex-German vessels. Then they took delivery of the *Naldera* and *Narkunda*, which had been launched in 1917 and 1918, but could not be completed because of wartime conditions. Then followed a new 'B' class for the Australian trade, and in 1922 the mail steamers *Moldavia* and *Mongolia* of around 16,300 tons.

P&O purchased a minority interest in the Orient Steam Navigation Co., and the British India Steam Navigation took control of the Eastern & Australian Mail Steam Ship Co. Frederick Green & Co. became associated with Anderson, Anderson & Co. in 1877. Anderson and Green became the Orient Steam Navigation Co. Ltd in 1878. The first ship to fly the company's house flag was the *Garonne*, which sailed for Australia in March of that year. *Orient II* was launched on 5 June 1878 and, costing around £150,000, she was the first ship expressly designed for the Australian mail service, the first ship to fulfil the Admiralty's requirements for an armed merchant cruiser in time of war and the first ship to be fitted with electricity. For the next seventeen years she ran regularly and with considerable success on the Australian mail run. She remained in service until 1910 and was sold after thirty years of sterling work. The *Ophir* was launched in 1891 and was the first twin-screw ship ever to go east of Suez; in 1901 she was chosen to convey the Duke and Duchess of Cornwall and York (King George V and Queen Mary) on their Empire Tour.

Following a closer association with Pacific Steam Navigation, it became the Orient-Pacific Line in 1901. Pacific Steam Navigation's interests were taken over by the Royal Mail Steam Packet Co. in 1906 and the company became the Orient-Royal Mail Line. When the Royal Mail Line withdrew in 1908 the company was renamed the Orient Line. Anderson and Green and Gray Davies & Co. amalgamated during the First World War as the Orient Line. During the war, when it faced wholesale requisition of its fleet, the line had difficulty in carrying on and became associated with the Inchcape Group. After the war the building of liners around 20,000 tons began, the *Orama* being the first. Her sister ship, the *Oronsay,* was constructed on the Clyde by John Brown & Co. *Otranto* followed in 1926, *Orford* in 1928, *Orontes* in 1929, *Orion* in 1935 and *Orcades* in 1937.

The General Steam Navigation Co. was purchased in 1920, and in 1923 the fleet rebuilding programme was postponed because of the increase in costs. *Mooltan* was introduced as the first P&O vessel to exceed 20,000 tons. She was joined by the *Viceroy of India* in 1929, which was the first large British passenger ship to have turbo-electric propulsion. The Australian service via the Cape was discontinued in December 1929 and the ships placed on the Suez Canal route. The chairman and managing director, Lord Inchcape, died in 1932, and the Moss Hutchison Line was purchased three years later. In 1936 the General Steam Navigation Co. acquired the fleet of the New Medway Steam Packet Co.

So successful was the electric drive of the *Viceroy of India* that similar machinery was adopted in the *Strathnaver* and *Strathaird* of 1931 and 1932 respectively, which were built for the Australian service. Then, in spite of the success and advantages of the turbo-electric drive, it was decided to go back to geared turbines for the *Carthage* and *Corfu* of 1931 for the Far Eastern service. In 1935 the *Strathmore* also entered service with geared turbines, and it was with this ship that the company decided to disregard public prejudice and give her only one funnel – previously it had been thought that a ship with two or more funnels was more likely to impress the travelling public. At the end of 1937 the *Stratheden* was completed also with steam turbines, and she was followed by her sister ship *Strathallan*, which was to become a war loss within a matter of four years. *Canton* was also completed prior to the outbreak of the Second World War, and she was an improvement on the *Carthage* and *Corfu*. Also completed in 1938 was the motor-ship *Ettrick*, which was intended for trooping services. She was not the first P&O motor-ship, for the cargo liners *Essex* and *Sussex* had been completed a couple of years earlier.

At the start of the Second World War the company's ships were immediately put on war footing. The Group owned 371 ships and they were located at sea and in various ports around the globe. P&O owned twenty-one passenger ships and fifteen cargo vessels, totalling 460,000 tons. Losses in the conflict ranged from the *Strathallan, Rawalpindi* and *Rajputana*, to various smaller units of the fleet. The company lost 182 vessels during the Second World War and a fleet replacement programme was agreed by the board. However, the increase in the use of commercial air travel and the surplus of war-built tonnage were factors that had to be considered in any long-term plan for the company. Liberty, Ocean and Empire ships had been built during the hostilities; these were relatively young and enabled the shipping industry to return to commercial operations at the end of the war.

When planning how best to replace their pre-war ships, it became apparent to P&O and Orient Lines that a repetition of the P&O Himalaya class and the Orient Line Orcades class, which started building shortly after the war, would be uneconomical. When these ships were built they were comparatively cheap and prices were much lower than they were ten years later. Replacement of these 22,000/28,000-ton ships of approximately 720 feet in overall length would have been too expensive in relation to their earning power. It would have been impossible to make them pay. The company decided to extend Australian voyages beyond Sydney across the Pacific and create a service linking Australia and New Zealand with the West Coast of North America via Suva and Honolulu. A decision was also made to extend Far East voyages so that they should link Hong Kong and Japan with the West Coast of North America. Triangular voyages were also envisaged in the Pacific to link Australia, the West Coast of America and the Far East, and Australia again. This was a completely new service with the Orient Line, covering the whole Pacific basin.

The first replacements to join the fleet were the cargo ships *Perim, Dongola* and *Devanha*. Himalaya was introduced in 1949, *Chusan* in 1950, and *Arcadia* and *Iberia* in 1954. *Arcadia* was the fourth vessel to be built at Clydebank for P&O and differed from *Iberia* in funnel styles, which were designed to keep exhaust smoke and gases from the decks. *Iberia* was built by Harland & Wolff at Belfast, and both were fitted with twin-screws driven by geared steam turbines providing a service speed of 22 knots. The Orient Line launched *Orcades* on 14 October 1947; *Oronsay* was introduced in 1951, *Orsova* in 1954 and *Oriana* in November 1960. *Orsova* was similar to *Oronsay* except that her overall length was increased by adding a curvature to the bow and extending the cruiser stern. Her accommodation provided for 681 first-class passengers and 813 tourist class, with a crew of 645. She was propelled by twin screws, driven by a set of geared turbines of Pametrada design, providing a service speed of 22 ½ knots.

During the 1950s the company decided to go into tanker owning, and the ships as they were delivered were allocated for operation by the various constituent members of the group. The first tanker was the *Lincoln*, which was completed in 1957 and sailed under the colours of the Federal Steam Navigation Co. Three of the tankers, *Derby*, *Maloja* and *Mantua*, were allocated to P&O under the ownership of the Charter Shipping Co. In 1954 the Orient Line started extending their Australian voyages across the Pacific via Suva and Honolulu to Vancouver, San Francisco and Los Angeles, and they combined with P&O in 1958 to form Orient and Pacific Lines. The aim was capture the American market both for the South Pacific routes to Australia and for the service across the Pacific to Japan and Hong Kong.

The following services operated under the name of Orient and Pacific Lines:

Panama Service: between Europe and the West Coast of America and Canada, via Panama, and from there across the Pacific to New Zealand and Australia or the Far East and vice versa.

South Pacific Service: connecting Australia, New Zealand, Suva, Honolulu, Canada and the U.S.A.

Japan–Australia Service: Between Australia, Manila, Hong Kong and Yokohama.

Japan–Pacific Service: Connecting Manila, Hong Kong, Yokohama, Honolulu, Canada and the U.S.A.

With the introduction of the passenger jet, aircraft travel by sea was no longer just a matter of transport between two places; it became a way of life and a pleasure, and attracted people who would use the service for a holiday or cruise. Passengers were attracted to the air of unhurried calm with which the ships and crews went about their business. Some would travel on a particular section of the voyage and others would travel around the world on a particular ship.

Canberra sailed on her maiden voyage from Southampton to Colombo, Melbourne and Sydney on 2 June 1961. She was 42,000 tons gross and was the largest passenger liner built in Great Britain since the first *Queen Elizabeth*. At the time she was introduced she could carry more passengers than any other ship in the world. Her passenger capacity was 2,238, of which 548 were first class and 1,690 tourist class. However, the numbers could vary as there were interchangeable cabins that accommodated two as first class and four as tourist class. Her superstructure above the weather deck was of aluminium and this was the largest to be fabricated, with a weight of over 1,100 tons. The use of lightweight aluminium allowed another superstructure deck to be fitted, and this extra space helped to increase her passenger capacity. *Canberra* also incorporated welded seams and butts and the hull was riveted to the frames.

Her propelling machinery was situated aft, allowing the centre of the ship to be devoted to passenger accommodation and facilities. The lifeboats were situated three decks down, giving an unobstructed view from the sports deck. She incorporated two separate decks of public rooms, three decks apart, with the restaurants being lower in the hull. She was designed so that the public rooms would be away from noisy areas and would offer quiet spaces for passengers. *Canberra* was built as a twin-screw turbo-electric ship, with machinery designed for 68,000 shp at 136.5 rpm in normal service. Her machinery enabled her to operate at a service speed of 27 ½ knots.

At the time of *Canberra*'s maiden voyage the P&O Group was the world's largest shipping company. Its fleet ranged from the *Canberra* to the *Royal Daffodil*, which took passengers on pleasure trips down the Thames. Among its 350 ships, comprising some 2,250,000 tons, were passenger liners, cargo vessels, oil tankers, tramps and troopships. Outside shipping the group had interests in the air, including Silver City Airways, and in the manufacture of refrigerators, lifts and air-conditioning plants. It was run by a board of sixteen directors, including five peers, Lord Bruce of Melbourne, Lord Geddes, Lord Inchcape, Lord Leathers and Lord Runciman. The total assets of the company amounted to £250 million and it was owned by 28,000 shareholders, with an average holding of £1,000. A trading profit (after depreciation) of around £10 million was made annually and a nett profit (after taxation) of £6 million. Shareholders received around £2 million a year in dividends and the group spent on average between £10 and £20 million on new ships to maintain its fleet.

Oriana was the last of the Orient Steam Navigation Co.'s ocean liners and was launched at the yard of Vickers Armstrong on 3 November 1959. She sailed on her maiden voyage from Southampton on 3 December 1959 to Australia, then on to the transpacific service from Sydney to Auckland, Vancouver and San Francisco. She was described as 'having a graceful hull in contrast with the superstructure and the flower-pot funnels'. She was built with transverse propulsion units at bow and stern, while her bulbous bow was believed to be the first fitted to a British passenger liner. She incorporated a mooring deck below the forecastle deck and, like *Canberra*, had lifeboats fitted below the boat deck. Accommodation was provided for 688 first-class passengers and 1,496 tourist class. She was fully air-conditioned and in first class and officers' accommodation the setting could be controlled by the occupant of the cabin. The public rooms, including staircases and entrances, was spread over eleven decks, of which the lower two had tourist accommodation only, and the upper two had first class only. Aluminium was also used in *Oriana* for the whole of the superstructure and the underdeck boat davits formed an integral part of the ship's structure. The davits differed from other gravity davits in that the trackways, which were attached to the deck head, had a straight run for the cradles. The lifeboats were built of fibreglass and were carried approximately 3 feet 6 inches over the shipside to give more space inboard. *Oriana* was propelled by twin-screws, each driven through double reduction gearing by a set of steam turbines of Pametrada design.

On 2 May 1960 P&O-Orient Lines (Passenger Services) Ltd was established to manage both fleets; in 1965 the company obtained the remaining minority shareholdings in the Orient Line and a plan was agreed to integrate the vessels of the two fleets. The following year P&O-Orient Line Ltd was changed to P&O and the managing company, P&O Orient Management Ltd, was renamed P&O Lines Management Ltd.

The *Carthage* and *Corfu* were sold to Japanese shipbreakers in 1961 and were replaced by the *Baudouinville* and *Jadotville*, which were built in 1956 for the Cia Maritime Belge (Lloyd Royal) SA; they were renamed *Cathay* and *Chitral*, respectively. Prior to *Canberra*'s maiden voyage on 2 June 1961, Sir Donald Anderson, chairman of P&O said,

> Any new passenger vessel must be designed to anticipate the future, if only because its "life" is twenty to thirty years. But there are special difficulties in reading the crystal ball as regards *Canberra* and, for that matter, her Orient Line consort, the 42,000 ton *Oriana*. How can anyone be certain that these ships will be sound investments throughout a period of profound changes, political, social, commercial and technological? How can the passenger vessel hope to withstand the challenge of jet aircraft. Has ocean travel any future at all. The answer is that ocean travel is not only a form of transport, it is also a holiday and a rest cure, a brief interlude of leisure, far from trials and tribulations.

Sir William Currie, former chairman of P&O added that, 'In an age of supersonic air travel to come, passenger ships will be convalescent homes for the weary air traveller. Ship-owners are plainly convinced that there will always be many people who prefer to take their time and who intend to enjoy travelling; that such people will naturally prefer the ship to the aeroplane; and that they will be sufficient in number to keep the up-to-date passenger liner profitably employed.' However, questions were asked why the firm should accept the commercial risk of a total investment of £30 million for the two passenger liners as the volume of traffic showed a pronounced seasonal variation. The P&O board felt that the solution was the expanding economy and resolved 'to widen their whole sphere of operations'.

In February 1971 an offer of £5.6 million in deferred stock was made by P&O for Coast Lines Ltd. This was accepted by the board, with Coast Lines and the General Steam Navigation Co. becoming P&O Short Sea Shipping, and later P&O Ferries. The Belfast Steamship Co. and Burns & Laird Lines became P&O Ferries Irish Sea Services from 1 October 1975. P&O took delivery of the *Spirit of London* in 1972, which was built by Cantieri Navali del Tirreno e Riuniti at Genoa. She was originally ordered by Klosters Rederi A/S (Norwegian Caribbean Lines) and was purchased on the stocks. She had accommodation for 730 passengers and was propelled by four diesel engines, which gave a service speed of 21 knots.

Chusan was used exclusively as a cruise ship from 1969, while *Himalaya* became popular in Australia after she undertook eight cruises between March and October 1968. *Himalaya* was replaced by *Arcadia* when she was sold for demolition in 1974. *Oriana* was designed to accommodate 638 first-class passengers and 1,496 in tourist class. *Canberra* could carry 556 first class and 1,616 passengers in tourist class. Both liners were transferred to P&O Cruises in 1973 when they were designated as one-class vessels with a passenger capacity of 1,700 berths.

Canberra and *Oriana* then provided Mediterranean, Caribbean and world cruises including fly-cruises from the United Kingdom. *Iberia* was sold for scrapping in 1972, *Chusan* in 1973, *Himalaya* and *Orsova* in 1974, *Nevasa* in 1975, *Oronsay* in 1975 and *Arcadia* in 1979.

Princess Cruises were taken over by P&O in 1974 from Stanley B. McDonald, who had founded the line by chartering the Canadian Pacific Alaska cruise ship *Princess Patricia* for Mexican Riviera cruises from Los Angeles. However, when the *Princess Patricia* proved unsuitable, the company used *Italia* for the service. She had been designed by Gustavo Finali and Romano Boico, who had created interiors for the Italian Line's *Augustus* and *Raffaello* and Home Line's *Oceanic* and *Homeric*. The charter was ended in 1973 and the Costa's Carla C replaced her. P&O purchased *Sea Venture* and *Island Venture*, renaming them *Pacific Princess* and *Island Princess*. Both vessels were the subject of a television series *The Love Boat* in 1977. *Spirit of London* was transferred and renamed *Sun Princess*. The acquisition of Princess Cruises enabled P&O to regain a foothold in the American cruise market, and the television series helped to create a new image for the cruise industry as 'fun ships', which was extended and reinforced by Ted Arison when he formed Carnival Cruise Lines. Prior to that there had been a rather formal approach to cruising that had limited its appeal, and the publicity from the television series gave people the opportunity to see another side to the industry.

In 1975 P&O was operating in five shipping divisions: Bulk Shipping Division (BSD), General Cargo (GCD), Passenger Division (Pass Div), European and Air Transportation Division (E&AT) and Energy Division (ED). The Swedish American liner *Kungsholm* was acquired in 1979 and renamed *Sea Princess*, with the new *Royal Princess* entering service in 1984.

The General Council of Shipping reported in 1982 that,

The passenger cruise ships of today are the successors to the passenger liners of the past. Though British deep sea cruise ships are now concentrated in the hands of only two owners, they are both efficient and successful operators, and their ten ships offer a range of cruises in all parts of the world. For those in a hurry to reach the sun, there are cruises which the passenger can fly out to join in the Mediterranean. One of the ships that offers this sort of cruise for part of the year is P&O's *Uganda*. The Cunard ships, led by the *Queen Elizabeth 2*, vary their programmes, but they are usually to be found in the Caribbean or off North America, normally on the Atlantic, but sometimes using Los Angeles as a base on the North American western seaboard. The three P&O "Princess" ships cruising out of US ports cover sharply contrasting regions: Mexico, Alaska and the Caribbean, or even the Polynesian world of the South Pacific. Australia is also a base for Oriana and, for part of the year by Canberra. These ships earn major sums of foreign currency for the United Kingdom, and their popularity has encouraged investment in new ships. *Canberra*, *Queen Elizabeth 2* and *Uganda* returned to the UK from the Task Force in the South Atlantic to their regular task of serving the thousands who believe that there is no better holiday in the world than cruising on a British passenger ship.

On 19 January 1987, P&O took over the European Ferries Group, who were trading as Townsend Thoresen. The group operated services from Dover, Portsmouth, Felixstowe and Cairnryan, and also included the ports of Felixstowe and Larne in Northern Ireland. The services were renamed P&O European Ferries on 22 October. Ten years later, P&O became the sole owner of North Sea Ferries and the group was later divided into P&O Portsmouth, P&O North Sea and a joint venture between P&O and the Stena Line as P&O Stena Line, in Dover. In August 2002, P&O acquired Stena Line's 40 per cent share of P&OSL, and it was merged with the Portsmouth and North Sea operations under the P&O Ferries Ltd brand. The Zeebrugge service was closed in 2002 and the Fleetwood–Larne route sold to Stena Line in 2004, together with the vessels in service.

It was announced in 1988 that P&O had acquired Sitmar Cruises and three new vessels that were under construction. The four ships operating in the Sitmar fleet were renamed *Dawn Princess*, *Fair Princess* and *Sky Princess*, with *Fairstar*, retaining her name, operating in the Australian market for P&O-Sitmar Cruises.

The new *Oriana* was introduced in 1995, with *Aurora* following in 2000 and *Ocean Princess* and *Sea Princess* moving to P&O cruises, becoming *Oceana* and *Adonia*. P&O Princess Cruises merged with the Carnival Corporation in 2003 and the new Arcadia was introduced in 2005, with *Royal Princess* moving to P&O Cruises, becoming *Artemis*. *Adonia* moved back to Princess and was renamed *Sea Princess*. *Ventura* entered service in 2008, *Artemis* was sold the following year and *Azura* joined the P&O Cruises fleet in 2010.

Carnival plc is the United Kingdom-listed company of the Carnival Group and was formed as a result of the merger between the Carnival Corporation and P&O Princess Cruises in 2003. P&O Princess remained a separate company and was subsequently relisted as Carnival plc. P&O Princess Cruises owned P&O Cruises, P&O Cruises Australia, Princess Cruises, Ocean Village and AIDA Cruises. Carnival UK also took control of the Cunard Line.

Windstar was sold to Ambassadors International Cruise Group and Swan Hellenic to Lord Sterling in 2007. Carnival comprises eleven individual shipping companies:

- AIDA Cruises, Germany
- Carnival Cruise Lines, United States
- Costa Cruises, Italy
- Cunard Line, United Kingdom
- Holland America Line, United States
- Ibero Cruises, Spain
- P&O Cruises, United Kingdom
- P&O Cruises Australia, Australia
- Princess Cruises, United States
- Seabourn Cruise Line, United States

The company also operated the Ocean Village Company from 2003 to 2010 with *Arcadia*, which was transferred and renamed *Ocean Village*. P&O Cruises (UK) vessels provided accommodation for 14,636 passengers with their seven ships. In 2012 *Arcadia*, *Adonia* and *Oriana* were advertised as adult-only ships, and in June 2011 the company announced an order for a 141,000-ton vessel that would be named *Britannia*. She was built by Fincantieri and entered service in 2015. She has capacity for 3,611 passengers and incorporates fourteen passenger decks and 1,819 cabins. The interior of the ship was designed by Richmond International, and her keel was laid at Trieste on 15 May 2013. *Britannia* was floated out of the dry dock on 14 February 2014.

In January 2014 the company announced plans to introduce a new fleet-wide livery based on the Union Flag, emphasising the company's British heritage. On 4 June 2015 P&O stated that *Adonia* would be transferred to Fathom, a new brand of the Carnival Corporation. Details of a new 180,000-ton ship were released on 5 September 2016, and she is expected to be delivered in 2020. She will be the largest cruise ship in the P&O Cruises fleet and would be designed for the British market. An order for the new vessel was placed with Meyer Werft at Papenburg, Germany, and she will be powered by Liquefied Natural Gas (LNG) in order to reduce air emissions.

The ship will feature a half-mile promenade deck incorporating cafés, restaurants and bars. There will be seventeen different dining options, including seven speciality restaurants and a pool suitable for any weather. The main pool will include a retractable stage, for use at night, and the swimming facilities will include four swimming pools and sixteen whirlpools on board. The large pool will include a giant glass-sky dome, which will be home to evening entertainment such as aerial performances. It is hoped that that the new ship will provide passengers with choice, flexibility and the ability to create individual holiday experiences, and the innovative use of space will offer an extensive range of dining, entertainment and relaxing areas. The new vessel will provide accommodation for 5,200 passengers, making it the largest ever built for the British cruise market. The Atrium will incorporate glass walls spanning three decks, which will enable natural light to flood in, and a grand staircase, gallery and overhead walkways will provide focal points.

Above: William Fawcett, 1829,
206 grt. 74 x 16 ft. 6 knots.
b. Fawcett, Preston & Company,
Liverpool. Caleb Smith, Liverpool.
Paddle steamer, single screw 60 IHP.

Right: Tagus, 1837, 783 grt. 193 x
26 x 17 ft. 9 ½ knots.
b. John Scott & Sons Ltd,
Cartsdyke, Greenock. Paddle
steamer, two cylinders, 286 IHP,
three boilers by Scott, Sinclair &
Co. Ltd. Passengers: eighty-six.

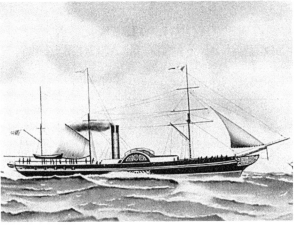

  At the time of her launch she
was the largest vessel built on
the River Clyde. In 1843 she
was placed on the London–
Constantinople route and was
rebuilt with accommodation for
passengers. She was chartered
to the Turkish government
in 1847 for trooping between
Constantinople and Salonika.
A further charter to T Hill at
Southampton took place in 1862.
She was sold and broken up by
Swan, Thompson & Moore two
years later.

Right below: Canton (1848/348 grt).

Above: *Mongolia*, 1865, 2,999 grt. 319 x 40 x 33 ft. 10 knots.
b. John Scott & Sons Ltd, Cartsdyke, Greenock. Single screw, two cylinders, 1,705 IHP by the Greenock Foundry Co. Passengers: 120 first class.
She was delivered for the Calcutta–Suez route and during her winter overhaul in 1873/74 new compound engines were fitted by Day Summers & Co. at Southampton. Her funnel was also heightened, and she was placed on the London–Bombay and Calcutta service and routes to Australia. She was transferred to the Venice–Bombay route in 1878 before being sold in 1888 and broken up.

Below: *Sunda*, 1866, 1,682 grt. 270 x 34 x 8 ft. 12 knots.
b. Backhouse & Dixon Ltd, Middlesbrough. Single screw, two cylinders, inverted, direct acting, 1,342 IHP, iron.
Ordered for Thomas Richardson & Sons Ltd, Hartlepool, and purchased on the stocks for the Hong Kong–Shanghai or Yokohama routes. In 1875, on a voyage from Hong Kong to Yokohama, she ran onto a reef and was beached. She was sold in 1882 to the Bombay agent of the Sultan of Zanzibar.

Above: *Tanjore*, 1865, 1,971 grt. 321 x 38 x 26 ft. 14 knots.

b. Thames Iron Works Ltd, London. Single screw, four cylinders, compound, tandem, direct acting by Miller Ravenhill & Co. Ltd, Blackwall, London. Iron.

The *Tanjore* was built for the Southampton–Marseilles–Alexandria service and achieved a speed of 17 knots on her official trials. Following this, *Ceylon, Columbian, China* and *Pera* were re-engined. She was fitted with new boilers and poop in 1870, and transferred to the Suez–Bombay route three years later. In 1876 she was re-engined by J. Howden & Co. at Glasgow, becoming compound inverted. She was used as a refugee ship at Alexandria in 1882 and laid up at Bombay six years later. In 1890 she was sold and operated on the Mecca pilgrimage trade.

Below: *Ballaarat*, 1882, 4,752 grt. 420 x 43 x 35 ft. 15 knots.

b. Caird & Coy. Ltd, Greenock. Single screw, two cylinders, compound inverted, 4,312 IHP, four double-ended boilers, by builders. Passengers: 160 first class, forty-eight second class. She was designed and built for the Southampton–Melbourne–Sydney route, and used as a troopship in China in 1900. She was sold in 1904, renamed *Laarat* and broken up.

Above: *Britannia*, 1887, 6,525 grt. 466 x 52 x 34 ft. 16 ½ knots.
b. Caird & Co. Ltd, Greenock. Single screw, high pressure, 7,000 IHP, 849 NHP, Four double-ended boilers by builders. Passengers: 250 first class, 160 second class.
On 18 October 1887 she ran aground in the River Thames on her delivery voyage and was refloated, undamaged. She left London on her maiden voyage to Colombo, Melbourne and Sydney on 5 November. In 1894 she ran aground in the Suez Canal and was chartered to the Admiralty in 1894/95, where she was operated as a troopship. She carried Prince Fushimi of Japan on his state visit to Britain. She was sold and broken up at Genoa in 1909.

Below: *Ophir*, 1891, 6,814 grt. 465 x 53 x 34 ft. 18 knots.
b. Robert Napier & Sons Ltd, Glasgow. Twin-screw, triple expansion, 1,398 IHP, five double- and two single-ended boilers by builder.
Built for the London–Suez–Melbourne-Sydney service and converted to an armed merchant cruiser in 1915. She was purchased by the Admiralty in 1918, becoming a hospital ship. She was laid up on the River Clyde in 1919 and broken up at Troon after three years.

Above: *Caledonia*, 1894, 7,558 grt. 486 x 54 x 35 ft. 18 knots.
b. Caird & Co. Ltd, Greenock. Single screw, triple expansion, five cylinders, 11,000 IHP, three double- and four single-ended boilers, by builder.
The *Caledonia* entered service with a white hull and yellow funnels and retained them for two years. In 1903 she was the first P&O vessel to use Tilbury Dock. She was mined off Marseilles in 1916 but returned to the Bombay service. She was sold in 1925 and broken up.

Below: *Egypt*, 1897, 7,912 grt. 500 x 54 x 33 ft. 16 knots.

Above: *Dongola*, 1905, 8,038 grt. 470 x 56 x 32 ft. 15 ½ knots.
b. Workman Clark & Co. Ltd, Belfast. Twin-screw, two quadruple expansion, 8,000 IHP, 2 double- and 4 single-ended boilers by builder.
She was originally used on trooping duties in India and made a record Southampton–Bombay voyage in eighteen days and seven hours in 1907. In 1911 she was present at the Coronation Naval Review and operated as a hospital ship in the Dardanelles in 1915. She collided with *Wimbledon* in the River Thames in 1920 and was beached. She undertook relief work at Yokohama, following the earthquake in 1923. She was sold and broken up in 1926.

Below: *Devanha*, 1906, 8,092 grt. 470 x 56 x 32 ft. 15 ½ knots.
b. Workman Clark & Co. Ltd, Belfast. Twin-screw, two quadruple expansion, 8,000 IHP, two double- and four single-ended boilers by builder. Passengers: 160 first class, eighty second class.
Devanha was delivered for the intermediate service to India and the Far East. She landed 12th Australian Battalion at Anzac Beach, Gallipoli, in 1915 and acted as a hospital ship with *Dongola*. She was the last vessel to leave the beaches. On 5 April 1916 she rescued the survivors of the British India Line's *Chantala* and later took them to Malta. She transferred to the Far East and Australian routes in 1919, and was sold and broken up in Japan in 1928.

Above: *Morea*, 1908, 10,895 grt. 562 x 61 x 24 ft. 16 knots.

b. Barclay Curle Ltd, Glasgow. Twin-screw, two quadruple expansion, 13,000 IHP, four single- and four double-ended boilers by builder. Passengers: 407 first class, 200 second class.

She was delivered for the London–Colombo–Melbourne route, but was converted to a troop carrier in 1915, and transported part of the Australian Expeditionary Force the following year. Requisitioned by the Admiralty in 1918 and converted to an Armed Merchant Cruiser, she was renamed HMS *Morea*. She returned to commercial service in 1919, and was employed on the Australian and Far East routes until 1930, when she was sold and broken up in Japan.

Below: *Borda*, 1914, 11,136 grt. 500 x 62 x 38 ft. 15 knots.

b. Caird & Co. Ltd, Greenock. Twin-screw, two quadruple expansion, 9,000 IHP, two double- and two single-ended boilers by builder. Passengers: 1,100 third class.

She sailed on her maiden voyage to Australia via the Cape on 27 March 1914, and later that year she was requisitioned by the Admiralty as a troopship. She returned to commercial service in 1920 and was laid up in 1928. She was sold and broken up in Japan two years later.

Above: *Mooltan*, 1923, 20,847 grt. 601 x 73 x 49 ft. 16 knots.

b. Harland & Wolff Ltd, Belfast. Twin-screw, two quadruple expansion, 16,000 IHP, six double- and two single-ended boilers by builder. Passengers: 327 first class, 329 second class. The *Mooltan* sailed on her maiden voyage from London to Colombo, Melbourne and Sydney on 21 December 1923. She was re-engined with geared turbines in 1929 (speed 17 knots) and was requisitioned by the Admiralty in 1939 and converted to an Armed Merchant Cruiser, with the top of the rear funnel removed. She was employed as a troopship in 1941 and was present at the landings at Arzeu on 11 November the following year. She returned to P&O service in 1948, with 1,030 tourist-class berths. She was sold in 1954 and broken up at Faslane.

Below: *Viceroy of India*, 1929, 19,648 grt. 612 x 76 x 42 ft. 19 knots.

b. Alexander Stephen & Sons Ltd. Twin-screw, two turbo electric, 17,000 SHP, six water tube boilers by builders. Electric motors by British Thomson Houston. Passengers: 415 first class, 258 second class.

She was ordered in 1927 as *Taj Mahal* and launched on 15 September the following year as *Viceroy of India*. In 1932 she achieved a crossing from London to Bombay in sixteen days, one hour and forty-two minutes. A swimming pool was fitted in 1938. She was requisitioned by the Admiralty in 1940 and used as a troopship. On 11 November 1942 she was torpedoed by *U-407* off Oran, Algeria, after landing troops and vehicles. Four people lost their lives.

P. & O. S.S. RAJPUTANA, 16,600 TONS GROSS.
India Mail and Passenger Service.

Above: Rajputana, 1925, 16,644 grt. 548 x 71 x 47 ft. 16 knots.

b. Harland & Wolff Ltd, Greenock. Twin-screw, two quadruple expansion, 15,000 IHP, six double-ended boilers by Harland & Wolff, Belfast. Passengers: 310 first class, 290 second class.

Rajputana was delivered for the Bombay service. Her engine was modified in 1930. On the outbreak of the Second World War she was at Yokohama and was sent to Esquimault, British Columbia. She was converted to an Armed Merchant Cruiser with one funnel. On 13 April 1941 she was torpedoed by *U-108*, west of Ireland. Forty-one people lost their lives.

Below: Orcades, 1903, 9,764 grt. 492 x 57 x 35 ft. 15 knots.

b. AG Vulkan, Stettin, Germany. Twin-screw, two quadruple expansion, 831 NHP by builders. Passengers: 123 first class, 476 third class.

Ordered and delivered as *Prinz Ludwig* for Norddeutscher Lloyd's Far Eastern route. She was surrendered to the United Kingdom in 1919 and managed by P&O. Purchased by the Orient Line in 1921, she was renamed *Orcades* and was broken up at Bremerhaven, Germany, in 1925.

Above: *Salsette*, 1908, 5,842 grt. 440 x 53 x 28 ft. 15 knots.

b. Caird & Co. Ltd, Greenock. Twin-screw, two quadruple expansion, 10,000 IHP by builder. Passengers: 100 first class, 120 second class.

Salsette was delivered for the Aden–Bombay service with a white hull, and from 1916 to 1917 she was employed on the London–Bombay–Colombo–Melbourne–Sydney service. On 20 July 1917 she was torpedoed near Portland Bill and sank in under an hour. Fifteen people lost their lives and the survivors were taken to Weymouth.

Below: *Macedonia*, 1904, 10,512 grt. 530 x 60 x 26 ft. 15 knots.

b. Harland & Wolff Ltd, Belfast. Twin-screw, two quadruple expansion, 13,000 IHP, five double- and two single-ended boilers by builder. Passengers: 377 first class, 187 second.

Macedonia sailed on her maiden voyage from London to Bombay on 12 February 1904 and was later transferred to the Australian route. Three years later she was operating on the London–China service and was requisitioned by the Admiralty in 1914 and converted to an Armed Merchant Cruiser. Later that year she and HMS *Bristol* were support ships at the Battle of the Falkland Islands, sinking the supply ships *Baden* and *Santa Isabel*. In 1916 she was sold to the Admiralty and was returned to commercial service on the Far East route in 1921. She was broken up in Japan in 1931.

S.S. "MACEDONIA."
10,512 Tons.

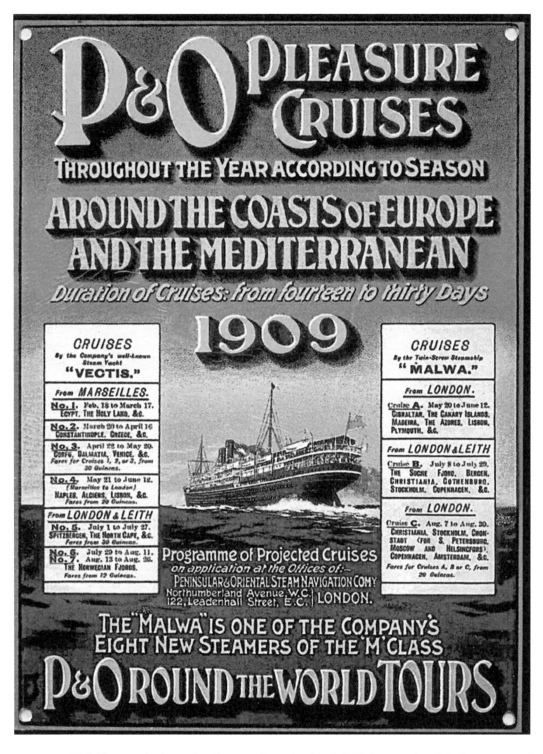

1909 P&O Pleasure Cruises advertisement featuring *Vectis* (1881/5,013 grt) and the 'new steamer' *Malwa* (1909/10,895 grt).

Above: *Moldavia*, 1903, 9,505 grt. 545 x 58 x 33 ft. 17 knots.

b. Caird & Co. Ltd, Greenock. Twin-screw, two triple expansion, three double and four single ended boilers by builders. Passengers: 348 first class, 166 second class.

She was the first of the 'M' class of ten ships ordered by the company for the Australian route. Following a shakedown cruise, she sailed on her maiden voyage on 11 December 1903 from London to Colombo, Melbourne and Sydney. She ran aground in 1907 on the Goodwin Sands but was floated off safely. Auckland was added to the route in 1911. She was requisitioned by the Admiralty in 1915 and converted to an Armed Merchant Cruiser. On 23 May 1918 she was torpedoed off Beachy Head and sank. Fifty-six people lost their lives.

Below: *Morea* (1908/10,895 grt).

Above: *Cathay* (2), 1925, 15,104 grt. 523 x 70 x 46 ft. 16 knots. b. Barclay Curle Ltd, Glasgow. Twin-screw, two quadruple expansion, 13,000 IHP, three double- and four single-ended boilers by builder. Passengers: 203 first class, 103 second class.

She was launched on 31 October 1924 by Lady Inchcape, wife of the P&O chairman, to operate on the Australian service. In 1939 she was converted to an Armed Merchant Cruiser and operated on the Bombay–Durban patrol, becoming a troopship in 1942. On 11 November 1942 she was bombed off Bougie, North Africa; an explosion blew off her stern and she sank.

Right: *Ranpura* (1925/16,688 grt) at full speed.

Above: An Orient liner leaves Sydney on a cruise.

Below: *Chitral* (1925/15,248 grt).

Above: Otranto (2) (1926/20,026 grt).

Below: Orsova (1909/12,026 grt).

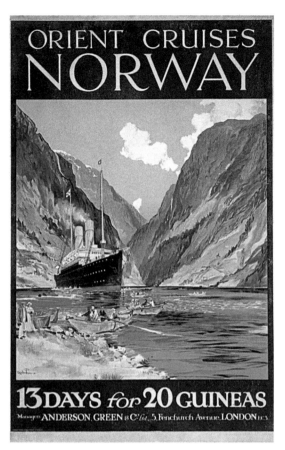

Left: Orient Cruises Norway advertisement.

Below: *Orontes* (2) (1929/20,097 grt).

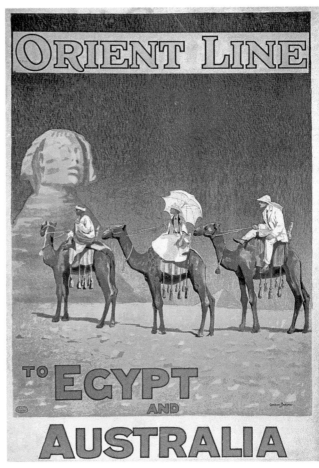

Above: *Orontes* sailing under the Sydney Harbour Bridge on 5 November 1930.

Right: Orient Line advertisement.

Above: *Corfu* (1931/14,251 grt).

Below: *Carthage* (2) (1931/14,304 grt).

Above: *Orontes* (2) (1929/20,097 grt).

Below: Deck games on *Oronsay* (1925/20,001 grt) in 1938.

1932 P&O Cruises advertisement.

Orford (1928/19,941 grt).

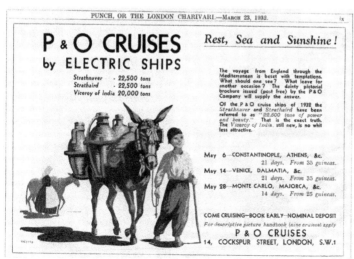

1932 P&O Cruises
by Electric Ships
advertisement.

Above: 1934 P&O Spring & Summer Cruises.

Right: P&O Pleasure Cruises 1934.

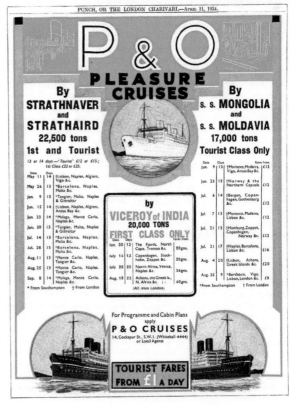

Viceroy of India cruise advertisement.

Above: *Strathnaver* (1931/22,270 grt).

Below: *Strathmore* (1935/23,580 grt).

A LIVING JEWEL

THE VICEROY OF INDIA IS COMMISSIONED FOR AN ATTRACTIVE ITINERARY, WHICH INCLUDES VISITS TO

DAKAR, RIO DE JANEIRO, SANTOS, CAPETOWN, LAS PALMAS & LISBON

FIRST CLASS ONLY
46 DAYS · FARES FROM 92 GNS.
FROM LONDON, 18th JAN., 1940

For all information apply : 14 Cockspur Street. S.W.I. 130 Leadenhall Street, E.C.3. Australia House. W.C.2, or local agents

1. Las Palmas.
2. Copacabana Beach, Rio de Janeiro.

Rio de Janeiro, again one of the high lights in the Viceroy of India's winter cruise itinerary, is an unforgettable spectacle either by day or by night. In the golden sunshine of warm, summer-like days, which make the English winter seem so much of another world, the beaches and superb mountain scenery hold a special allure, whilst by night the lights glittering round the coast like a string of diamonds, tell of the City's night life with all its gaiety and sophistication.

The Viceroy of India, with her fine accommodation, sun and sports decks and open-air swimming pool, is a confirmed favourite with regular travellers. Among ports to be visited are Santos, which vies with Rio in its lovely beaches and the gay life of its casinos, and Capetown, basking in summer sunshine.

P&O *Viceroy of India* WINTER CRUISE · 1940

Left: A 'Living Jewel' cruise advertised on the *Viceroy of India*, which was due to sail from London on 18 January 1940 to Dakar, Rio de Janeiro, Santos, Cape Town, Las Palmas and Lisbon. However, other events took precedence and she was converted to a troopship in 1940. She was torpedoed and sunk by *U-407* off Oran, Algeria, on 11 November 1942.

Below: *Orcades* (2) 1937/23,456 grt).

Above: *Stratheden*, 1937, 23,732 grt. 665 x 82 x 36 ft. 20 knots.
b. Vickers Armstrong Ltd, Barrow. Twin-screw, six single reduction geared turbines, 24,000 SHP, four water tube boilers by builder. Passengers: 530 first class, 450 tourist. She served as a troopship during the Second World War and returned to commercial service in 1947. In 1950 she made four round voyages on charter to the Cunard Line and was converted to a one-class ship in 1961. Following her last voyage for P&O she was chartered to the Travel Savings Association in 1963, and was sold to John S. Latsis the following year. She was renamed *Henrietta Latsis Marianna Latis* in 1966 and was broken up at Spezia in 1969.

Right: Sports deck on *Stratheden*.

Canton (4) (1938/15,784 grt).

Carthage (2)
(1931/14,304 grt).

Strathmore.

Above: *Strathmore* (1935/23,580 grt).

Below: *Strathmore* first class lounge.

Above: *Strathmore* first-class Verandah café.

Below: *Strathmore* tourist-class smoking room.

Above: *Strathnaver* (1931/22,270 grt).

Below: *Strathaird* (1932/22,544 grt) at Brisbane, Australia.

Above: *Stratheden* (1937/23,732 grt).

Below: *Himalaya* (3) (1949/27,955 grt). (Barry Eagles)

Above: *Chusan* (3) (1950/24,215 grt). (Barry Eagles)

Below: *Chusan* (1950/24,215 grt).

FAR EASTERN FREIGHT SERVICES SCHEDULE OF OUTWARD SAILINGS

Hamburg Rotterdam Antwerp Grangemouth Middlesbrough London Southampton

VESSEL	SAILING FROM							DUE AT							
	Hamburg	Rotterdam	Antwerp	Grangemt'h	M'brough	London	So'ton	Penang	Port Swettenham	Singapore	Bangkok	Manila	Hong Kong	Japan	China
CORFU						1 Feb	3 Feb	26 Feb		27 Feb			5 Mar		
SOMALI		21 Jan	26 Jan	30 Jan		8 Feb		7 Mar		2 Mar		14 Mar	17 Mar	23 Mar	
SALSETTE		22 Feb	4 Feb			19 Feb	24 Feb	21 Mar	24 Mar	29 Mar	4 Apr	18 Apr	10 Apr		
CHITRAL						28 Feb	2 Mar	24 Mar		25 Mar			31 Mar		
SINGAPORE	9 Feb	21 Feb	23 Feb	27 Feb		7 Mar		7 Apr	2 Apr	28 Mar		14 Apr	17 Apr	23 Apr	
CHUSAN						11 Mar		31 Mar		2 Apr		7 Apr	9 Apr	17 Apr	
CANTON						28 Mar	30 Mar	22 Apr		24 Apr			30 Apr		
SALMARA	23 Feb	17 Mar	14 Mar			30 Mar		25 Apr		27 Apr	3 May	18 May	9 May		
SUNDA	11 Mar	20 Mar	22 Mar	26 Mar		7 Apr		8 May	3 May	28 Apr		15 May	18 May	24 May	
CATHAY						12 Apr	14 Apr	7 May		8 May			14 May	20 May	
COROMANDEL	25 Mar	30 Apr	12 Apr			27 Apr	2 May	30 May		1 June	8 June	18 June	14 June		
SOUDAN	8 Apr	22 Apr	24 Apr	28 Apr		7 May		7 June	2 June	28 May		14 June	17 June	23 June	
CHITRAL						17 May	19 May	10 June		11 June			17 June	23 June	
CANNANORE	19 Apr	28 May	7 May			25 May	30 May	29 June		1 July	8 July	18 July	14 July		

With liberty to call at any ports on or off the route and to proceed via Suez, Cape or Panama. The route and date of sailing is subject to change or alteration with or without notice. No cargo to be forwarded without engagement. Refrigerated space available on all vessels. For further details of closing dates and conditions of carriage please see the current sailing cards.

P & O — ORIENT MANAGEMENT LTD.
122 Leadenhall Street, London, EC3. Telephone Avenue 8000. Telex 28624 London

ESCOMBE McGRATH & CO. LTD.
Freight Brokers in the United Kingdom. 4 Lloyds Avenue, London, EC3. Telephone Royal 9181. Telex 28306 London
Also at Birmingham, Grimsby, Immingham, Glasgow, Liverpool, Manchester, Middlesbrough and Southampton

Above: P&O sailing schedule, 1961.

Below: *Chusan* postcard.

P. & O. 'CHUSAN'
1st Class Public Rooms

Chusan (3), 1950, 24,215 grt. 673 x 85 x 36 ft. 23 knots.
b. Vickers Armstrong Ltd, Barrow. Twin-screw, six double reduction geared steam turbines, 42,500 SHP, four water tube boilers by builder. Passengers: 474 first class, 514 tourist.
A Thornycroft cowl was added to the funnel in 1951. It was sold in 1973 and broken up at Taiwan.

Left: *Stratheden* and *Strathmore* brochure, 1960.

Below: *Orion* (1935/23,371 grt).

Above: *Orcades* (3) (1948/28,472 grt).

Below: *Oronsay* (2) (1951/28,136 grt). (Barry Eagles)

Above: P&O Cruise advertisement.

Below: *Oronsay* (2) in white livery in 1963. (Barry Eagles)

Above: *Orsova* (2) (1954/29,091 grt). (Barry Eagles) *Below*: Orient Line Cruises and Fares, 1955.

SUMMARY OF CRUISES

The Orient Line have pleasure in announcing the following Cruises during 1955 by S.S. "ORSOVA," 29,000 tons; S.S. "ORCADES," 28,000 tons and S.S. "ORION," 24,000 tons :—

CRUISE No.	SHIP	DATE	PORTS OF CALL
28	ORCADES	24th June for 21 days	London (Tilbury), Palma, Messina for Taormina, Athens, Limassol (Cyprus), Beirut for Baalbek and Damascus, Rhodes, Palermo, Algiers, Southampton.
29	ORION	9th July for 13 days	London (Tilbury), Lisbon for Cintra and Estoril, Gibraltar, Palma, Algiers, Casablanca for Rabat, Corunna for Santiago de Compostela, Southampton.
30	ORCADES	16th July for 13 days	Southampton, Gibraltar, Spezia for Pisa and Florence, Palma, Casablanca for Rabat, Corunna for Santiago de Compostela, Southampton.
31	ORION	23rd July for 9 days	Southampton, Bergen, Oslo, Gothenburg, Amsterdam, London (Tilbury).
32	ORCADES	30th July for 13 days	Southampton, Vigo, Ceuta for Tetuan, Cannes, Santa Margherita for Rapallo and Portofino, Lisbon for Cintra and Estoril, London (Tilbury).
33	ORSOVA	30th July for 13 days	London (Tilbury), Bergen, Aandalsnaes, Merok, Copenhagen, Hamburg, Amsterdam, Southampton.
34	ORSOVA	13th August for 21 days	Southampton, Lisbon for Cintra and Estoril, Palma, Messina for Taormina, Rhodes, Athens, Dubrovnik, Venice, Ajaccio, Vigo, Southampton.

FIRST CLASS FARES

TYPE OF CABIN	CRUISE No.						
	28	29	30	31	32	33	34
	£	£	£	£	£	£	£
Air-Conditioned Flat	565	—	375	—	375	350	565
Suite	—	300	—	210	—	—	—
Special Staterooms	445 465	260	285 300	180	285 300	285 300	470 490
Single berth Cabins	137 to 177	83 to 109	89 to 117	58 to 75	89 to 117	103 to 124	167 to 200
Outside twin-bedded Cabins (per berth)	147 to 177	89 to 109	96 to 117	62 to 75	96 to 117	96 to 124	156 to 200
Outside two-berth Cabins (per berth)	127 to 147	71 to 83	82 to 96	49 to 58	82 to 96	82 to 103	134 to 167
Air-Conditioned Inside two-berth Cabins (per berth)	127	—	82	—	82	82 89	134 145
Inside two-berth Cabins (per berth)	107 117	66 71	69 75	45 49	69 75	69 75	112 123
Private Bathroom supplement	44	27	27	18	27	27	44
Private Shower supplement	—	—	—	—	—	17	26

TOURIST CLASS FARES

TYPE OF CABIN	CRUISE No.						
	28	29	30	31	32	33	34
	£	£	£	£	£	£	£
Single berth Cabins	64 to 77	39 to 50	41 to 49	27 to 36	41 to 49	46	71
Two-berth Cabins (per berth)	64 to 82	39 to 50	41 to 52	27 to 36	41 to 52	41 to 52	64 to 82
Three-berth Cabins (per berth)	57 71	36 to 46	37 46	24 to 33	37 46	46 to 52	71 to 82
Four-berth Cabins (per berth)	—	—	—	—	—	46 49	71 77

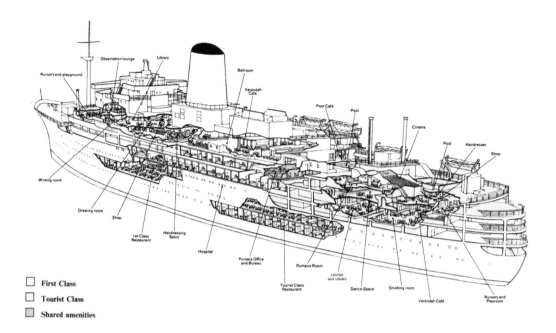

Arcadia (2), 1954, 29,664 grt. 721 x 91 x 40 ft. 22 knots.
b. John Brown & Co. Ltd, Clydebank. Twin-screw, six double and single reduction geared steam turbines, 42,500 IHP, three water tube boilers by builder. Passengers: 679 first class, 735 tourist. (Barry Eagles)

Above: *Iberia* (3), 1954, 29,614 grt. 719 x 91 x 40 ft. 22 knots. b. Harland & Wolff Ltd, Belfast. Twin-screw, six double and single reduction geared steam turbines, 42,500 IHP, three water tube boilers by builder. Passengers: 679 first class, 735 tourist. (Barry Eagles)

Right: *Iberia* (3) sports deck.

CANBERRA

MAIDEN
VOYAGE 2ND
JUNE
1961

P.O - ORIENT LINES

Canberra (1961/45,270 grt) maiden voyage brochure.

CANBERRA MAIDEN VOYAGE

	1961	HOMEWARD CONNECTIONS
leave Southampton	June 2	
Gibraltar	June 4	
Naples	June 6	*leave Naples June 11-London June 18 STRATHAIRD*
Port Said	June 9	
Aden	June 12	
Colombo	June 16	*leave Colombo June 25-London July 16 STRATHEDEN*
Fremantle	June 22	
Melbourne	June 25–27	
Sydney	June 28	*leave Sydney June 30-London Aug. 6 . . . IBERIA*
		(via East Africa)
leave Sydney	July 1	
Auckland	July 4	
Honolulu	July 10–11	*leave Honolulu July 17-London Aug. 30*
		(via Far East) HIMALAYA
Vancouver	July 15–16	
San Francisco	July 18–20	*leave San Francisco Aug. 13-London Oct. 16*
		(via Far East and Sydney) ORSOVA*
Los Angeles	July 21–22	
Honolulu	July 26	
Wellington	Aug. 3	
Sydney	Aug. 6	

OUTWARD CONNECTIONS

ORCADES. London July 5-Sydney Aug. 4   *leave* Sydney   Aug. 8
                                            Melbourne   Aug. 9–10
                                            Fremantle   Aug. 13

CORFU. Southampton July 22-Colombo Aug. 10 leave Colombo   Aug. 18
                                            Aden   Aug. 22
                                            Port Said   Aug. 26

ORIANA. Southampton Aug. 6-Naples Aug. 10   *leave* Naples   Aug. 28

ORONTES. London Aug. 16-Naples Aug. 22   *leave* Naples   Aug. 28

ORONTES. London Aug. 16-Gibraltar Aug. 19 leave Gibraltar   Aug. 30

ORONSAY. London Aug. 15-Lisbon Aug. 18
                                      arrive Southampton   Sep. 1

*Itinerary based on anticipated delivery date, any
change in which may necessitate amendments to
the programme.*

FIRST CLASS
Swimming Pool
and Sun Deck

Above: *Canberra* at Sydney.

Below: *Oriana*'s launch at Vickers Armstrong, Barrow, 3 November 1959.

Above: *Oriana* (1960/41,910 grt) at Southampton. (Barry Eagles)

Below: Cunard liner *Carmania* and *Chusan*.

Above: *Canberra* on a Caribbean cruise.

Below: *Princess Patricia* (1949/5,611 grt) in Canadian Pacific Railway service.

Spirit of London (1972/17,370 grt) on the slipway at Cantieri Navali del Tirreno e Riuniti, Riva Trigoso, Italy.

Island Princess (1971/20,186 grt).

Discovery (ex-*Island Princess*) operated for Voyages of Discovery between 2002 and 2013.

Above: *Spirit of London* (1972/17,370 grt).

Below: *Canberra* anchored off the Falkland Islands.

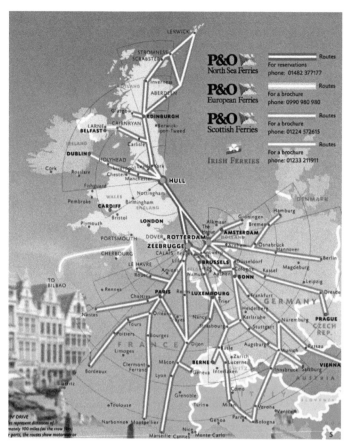

P&O
North Sea Ferries

Routes
For reservations
phone: 01482 377177

P&O
European Ferries

Routes
For a brochure
phone: 0990 980 980

P&O
Scottish Ferries

Routes
For a brochure
phone: 01224 572615

IRISH FERRIES

Routes
For a brochure
phone: 01233 211911

Left: P&O Ferries routes.

Below: *Fairwind*
(1957/21,989 grt).

Above: *Fairwind* in 1987.

Below: *Royal Princess* (1984/44,588 grt).

Above: *Oriana* (1995/69,153 grt).

Below: *Aurora* (2000/ 76,152 grt).

Above: *Ventura* (2008/116,017 grt). (Barry Eagles)

Below: *Oceana* (1999/77,499 grt). (Barry Eagles)

Above: *Adonia* (2001/30,277 grt).

Below: *Britannia* (2015/143,730 grt).

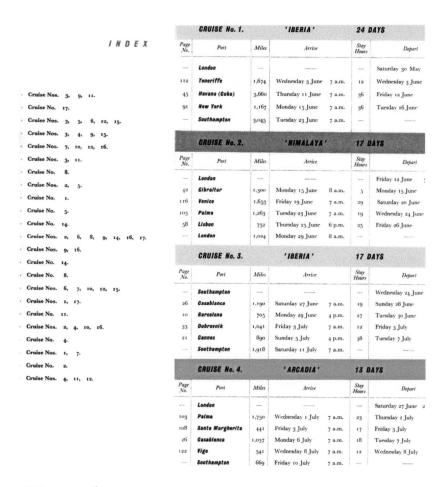

CRUISE No. 1. 'IBERIA' 24 DAYS

Page No.	Port	Miles	Arrive	Stay Hours	Depart
—	London	—	——	—	Saturday 30 May
112	Teneriffe	1,674	Wednesday 3 June 7 a.m.	12	Wednesday 3 June
45	Havana (Cuba)	3,660	Thursday 11 June 7 a.m.	36	Friday 12 June
91	New York	1,167	Monday 15 June 7 a.m.	36	Tuesday 16 June
—	Southampton	3,045	Tuesday 23 June 7 a.m.	—	——

CRUISE No. 2. 'HIMALAYA' 17 DAYS

Page No.	Port	Miles	Arrive	Stay Hours	Depart
—	London	—	——	—	Friday 12 June
42	Gibraltar	1,300	Monday 15 June 8 a.m.	5	Monday 15 June
116	Venice	1,653	Friday 19 June 7 a.m.	29	Saturday 20 June
103	Palma	1,263	Tuesday 23 June 7 a.m.	19	Wednesday 24 June
58	Lisbon	752	Thursday 25 June 6 p.m.	25	Friday 26 June
—	London	1,024	Monday 29 June 8 a.m.	—	——

CRUISE No. 3. 'IBERIA' 17 DAYS

Page No.	Port	Miles	Arrive	Stay Hours	Depart
—	Southampton	—	——	—	Wednesday 24 June
26	Casablanca	1,190	Saturday 27 June 7 a.m.	19	Sunday 28 June
10	Barcelona	705	Monday 29 June 4 p.m.	27	Tuesday 30 June
33	Dubrovnik	1,041	Friday 3 July 7 a.m.	12	Friday 3 July
21	Cannes	890	Sunday 5 July 4 p.m.	38	Tuesday 7 July
—	Southampton	1,918	Saturday 11 July 7 a.m.	—	——

CRUISE No. 4. 'ARCADIA' 13 DAYS

Page No.	Port	Miles	Arrive	Stay Hours	Depart
—	London	—	——	—	Saturday 27 June 2
103	Palma	1,750	Wednesday 1 July 7 a.m.	23	Thursday 2 July
108	Santa Margherita	441	Friday 3 July 7 a.m.	17	Friday 3 July
26	Casablanca	1,037	Monday 6 July 7 a.m.	18	Tuesday 7 July
122	Vigo	541	Wednesday 8 July 7 a.m.	12	Wednesday 8 July
—	Southampton	669	Friday 10 July 7 a.m.	—	——

P&O cruise sailings, 1959.

CRUISE No. 5.

Page No.	Port	Miles	Arrive	Stay Hours	Depart
—	Southampton	—	——	—	Saturday 11 July 1 p.m.
21	Cannes	1,918	Wednesday 15 July 6 p.m.	25	Thursday 16 July 7 a.m.
42	Gibraltar	732	Saturday 18 July Noon	7	Saturday 18 July 7 p.m.
40	Las Palmas	700	Monday 20 July 8 a.m.	11	Monday 20 July 7 p.m.
—	Southampton	1,550	Friday 24 July 7 a.m.	—	——

CRUISE No. 9.

Page No.	Port	Miles	Arrive	Stay Hours	Depart
—	Southampton	—	——	—	Saturday 1 August 1 p.m.
60	Madeira	1,535	Tuesday 4 August 8 a.m.	22	Wednesday 5 August 6 a.m.
26	Casablanca	472	Thursday 6 August 8 a.m.	11	Thursday 6 August 7 p.m.
10	Barcelona	705	Saturday 8 August 8 a.m.	22	Sunday 9 August 6 a.m.
58	Lisbon	817	Tuesday 11 August 7 a.m.	23	Wednesday 12 August 6 a.m.
—	Southampton	890	Friday 14 August 7 a.m.	—	——

CRUISE No. 6. 'IBERIA' 13 DAYS

Page No.	Port	Miles	Arrive	Stay Hours	Depart
—	Southampton	—	——	—	Saturday 18 July 1 p.m.
81	Naples	2,145	Thursday 23 July 7 a.m.	23	Friday 24 July 6 a.m.
21	Cannes	408	Saturday 25 July 7 a.m.	19	Sunday 26 July 2 a.m.
58	Lisbon	1,054	Tuesday 28 July 8 a.m.	22	Wednesday 29 July 6 a.m.
—	Southampton	890	Friday 31 July 7 a.m.	—	——

CRUISE No. 10. 'CHUSAN' 13 DAYS

Page No.	Port	Miles	Arrive	Stay Hours	Depart
—	Southampton	—	——	—	Saturday 8 August 1 p.m.
103	Palma	1,616	Wednesday 12 Aug. 7 a.m.	16	Wednesday 12 Aug. Midn't.
81	Naples	581	Friday 14 August 7 a.m.	41	Saturday 15 August Midn't.
30	Ceuta	979	Tuesday 18 August 7 a.m.	11	Tuesday 18 August 6 p.m.
—	Southampton	1,166	Friday 21 August 7 a.m.	—	——

CRUISE No. 7. 'ARCADIA' 14 DAYS

Page No.	Port	Miles	Arrive	Stay Hours	Depart
—	Southampton	—	——	—	Saturday 25 July 1 p.m.
30	Ceuta	1,166	Tuesday 28 July 7 a.m.	11	Tuesday 28 July 6 p.m.
81	Naples	979	Thursday 30 July 6 p.m.	25	Friday 31 July 7 p.m.
112	Teneriffe	1,694	Tuesday 4 August 8 a.m.	16	Tuesday 4 August Midn't
—	Southampton	1,550	Saturday 8 August 7 a.m.	—	——

CRUISE No. 11. 'IBERIA' 15 DAYS

Page No.	Port	Miles	Arrive	Stay Hours	Depart
—	Southampton	—	——	—	Saturday 15 August 1 p.m.
100	Palermo	2,080	Thursday 20 August 7 a.m.	10	Thursday 20 August 5 p.m.
33	Dubrovnik	483	Friday 21 August 6 p.m.	19	Saturday 22 August 1 p.m.
10	Barcelona	1,041	Monday 24 August 5 p.m.	26	Tuesday 25 August 7 p.m.
122	Vigo	1,035	Friday 28 August 7 a.m.	12	Friday 28 August 7 p.m.
—	Southampton	669	Sunday 30 August 7 a.m.	—	——

CRUISE No. 8. 'CHUSAN' 13 DAYS

Page No.	Port	Miles	Arrive	Stay Hours	Depart
—	London	—	——	—	Saturday 25 July 2.30 p.m.
37	Genoa	2,147	Thursday 30 July 8 a.m.	18	Friday 31 July 2 a.m.
77	Messina	486	Saturday 1 August 7 a.m.	11	Saturday 1 August 6 p.m.
58	Lisbon	1,515	Tuesday 4 August 1 p.m.	17	Wednesday 5 August 6 a.m.
—	Southampton	890	Friday 7 August 7 a.m.	—	——

CRUISE No. 12. 'ARCADIA' 13 DAYS

Page No.	Port	Miles	Arrive	Stay Hours	Depart
—	Southampton	—	——	—	Saturday 15 August 1 p.m.
81	Naples	2,145	Thursday 20 August 7 a.m.	12½	Thursday 20 August 7.30 p.m.
21	Cannes	375	Saturday 22 August 5 p.m.	25	Saturday 22 August 6 p.m.
30	Ceuta	752	Monday 24 August 8 a.m.	18	Tuesday 25 August 2 a.m.
122	Vigo	520	Wednesday 26 August 7 a.m.	12	Wednesday 26 August 7 p.m.
—	Southampton	669	Friday 28 August 7 a.m.	—	——

Above: *Oriana*, 1960,
41,910 grt.
804 x 97 x 32 ft. 23 knots.
b. Vickers Armstrong Ltd,
Barrow. Twin-screw, six
double reduction geared
steam turbines, four water
tube boilers by builder.

Left: *Oriana* on speed
trials, P&O Cruises.

Right: *Canberra*, 1961, 45,270 grt.
819 x 102 x 42 ft. 27 knots.
b. Harland & Wolff Ltd, Belfast.
Twin-screw, two steam turbines,
88,200 BHP, three water tube boilers
by builder. Passengers: 548 first
class, 1690 tourist. P&O Cruises.

Below: Looking down on the bow of
Canberra. (Barry Eagles)

Above: *Canberra* and the tug *Sealyham*. (Barry Eagles)

Below: *Canberra* berthed astern of a Russian cruise ship. (Barry Eagles)

P&O 'We discover cruising'
advertisement.

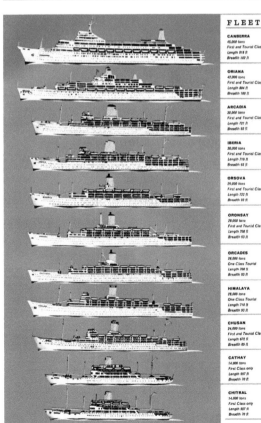

P&O cruising fleet, 1967. (P&O)

Left: P&O Cruises advert featuring *Oriana*.

Below: *Oriana* (1960/41,910 grt) in the Panama Canal.

P&O Sailing details.

Above: 1961 P&O Sailing details. *Below*: *Canberra* and *Oriana* in dry dock.

Cathay, 1957, 13,531 grt. 558 x 70 x 41 ft. 16 ½ knots.

b. Anon Cockerill-Ougree, Hoboken. Single screw, double reduction geared Parsons turbine, 12,500 BHP, three water tube boilers by builders. Passengers: 274 first class.

Delivered to Compagnie Maritime Belge, Antwerp, as *Baudouinville* and purchased by P&O in 1961, she was then renamed *Cathay*. She was transferred to the Eastern & Australian Steam Ship Co. in 1970, operating on the Australia–Japan route. She was sold to the Republic of China in 1976, becoming *Shanghai*. (Barry Eagles)

Above: British India Line's educational cruise ship *Devonia* (1939/11,275 grt).

Below: Educational cruise ship *Dunera* (1937/11,197 grt).

Above: *Nevasa* (1956/20,527 grt) berths at Liverpool Landing Stage.

Below: *Uganda* deck plan.

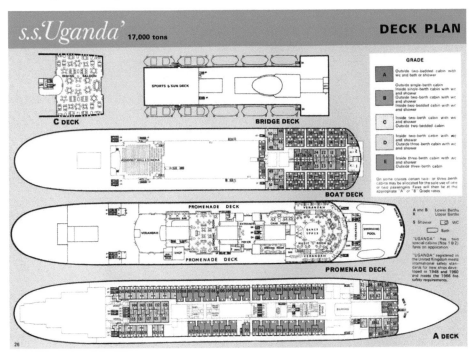

COACH AND CRUISE
HOLIDAYS 1969
WITH P&O

P&O Coach and Cruise holidays in 1969.The Coach and Cruise holidays offered a package to passengers who preferred to travel by road to their cruise holiday in the Mediterranean. A coach would take passengers across the Channel from Southampton and through France and Italy, where they would join *Arcadia, Chusan* or *Iberia* for the cruise. The holidays normally combined five to six days overland by coach with a six- to eight-day Mediterranean cruise.

How to have two holidays at the same time. That's what you do with the new P&O Coach and Cruise idea.

And what a way to go!

Head for the 'Med' across France in a luxury coach. Stop for an evening in Paris maybe. Drive on under the relaxing blue skies and lazy continental sun. See Montreux, Como, Naples and—well, you'll see what you'll see when you flick through the following pages. Then, deep down on the Mediterranean coast, where you'd normally turn round and start back, you start holiday number two instead. You board your great white P&O cruise liner and you're off and away. On board, there are restaurants, swimming pools, bars, lounges, sun decks—everything. Just relax and have the time of your life. Call at exciting ports. Go souvenir hunting. Do everything, do nothing. But cruising you will love. It's your very own world of sun, sea and excitement.

That's coaching and cruising. But if you prefer, you can cruise first and coach back. Either way, it's the holiday of a lifetime!

1 The 30,000 ton *Arcadia* at Venice
2 The 24,000 ton *Chusan* at Malta
3 Sun and sea breezes
4 The 30,000 ton *Iberia* bound for the sun
5 Paris—The Opéra
6 The coach for your overland tour

Arcadia (2) and *Arcadia* (3) in the River Mersey. Although *Arcadia* (2) operated mainly from Southampton, she did make occasional visits to the Mersey following annual overhaul by Harland & Wolff at Belfast. *Arcadia* (3) is shown on a 'Round Britain' cruise, leaving the Liverpool Cruise Terminal.

Special Farewell Cruise of 'Chusan'

17–26 March 1973
10 days—Fly/Cruise No. 550

From £79 Tourist   £125 First

We have arranged this short holiday especially for a limited number of our regular CHUSAN passengers who will not want to miss this last opportunity to sail in CHUSAN before she leaves the cruising scene.

Depart by air, morning Sat 17 March from *London (Gatwick)* to *Teneriffe*. Transfer to Semiramis Hotel, Puerto de la Cruz and stay nights of 17 and 18 March. Optional excursion Sun 18 Mar. Transfer to CHUSAN morning Mon 19 March.

Teneriffe
Dep 14.00 Mon 19 March
Las Palmas
Arr 19.00 Mon 19 March stay 6 hrs.
Lanzarote
Arr 09.00 Tues 20 March stay 8 hrs.
Madeira
Arr 09.00 Wed 21 March stay 17 hrs.
Lisbon
Arr 08.00 Fri 23 March stay 18 hrs.
Southampton
Arr morning Mon 26 March.

For details of Fares etc., see page 43

Chusan 24,000 tons

Special Farewell Cruise of 'Chusan'—17 March

Full details of the itinerary for Chusan's Farewell Cruise will be found on page 23 and should be read in conjunction with the fares and information that follow.

FARES

First Class
Single cabins with private facilities £175.
Single cabins £170.
Two-bedded cabins with private facilities £155.
Two-bedded cabins £145.
Two-berth cabins with private facilities £145.
Two-berth cabins £125.

Tourist Class
Two-berth cabins with private facilities £109.
Two-berth cabins £99.
Four-berth cabins £79.
(Air fare content subject to Government approval).

Included in your fare is:—
Swift jet travel from London (Gatwick) to Teneriffe, two days at the 5-star luxury SEMIRAMIS HOTEL in Puerto de la Cruz, plus all meals (except lunch) including a 'welcome' cocktail party and candlelight gala dinner—all specially arranged for our 'CHUSAN Club' passengers.

1 Supplement for single room (limited) at Semiramis Hotel £5.50 (for two nights).
2 Meals at hotel include English breakfast and dinner but not lunch.
3 A Southampton/Teneriffe sea port tax of £3.25 per adult is payable in addition to all fares.
4 Free air baggage allowance 44 lbs. (20 kilos).

If you want to be one of the lucky ones aboard *Chusan* in March just complete the Application Form on page 47.

Details of the 'Special Farewell Cruise' of *Chusan* in March, 1973.

P&O's Southern Ferries service from Southampton to Portugal and North Africa.

Royal Princess (1984/44,588 grt) was the first purpose-built cruise ship to be built for the P&O Group.

The World's Most Advanced Cruise Ship

=== THE ROYAL PRINCESS ===

Mediterranean & Scandinavia 1989

=== 12/14 night holidays from £1264 ===

Advance programme details

P&O Group

P&O Ferries' 150 years of P&O.

Sitmar Line's *Fairsky* became *Sky Princess* in 1988, *Pacific Sky* in 2000, *Sky Wonder* in 2006, *Atlantic Star* in 2009 and *Antic* in 2013. She arrived at Aliaga on 14 April 2013 and was broken up.

Left: *Fairsea* (1956/21,947 grt).

Below: In 1988 P&O acquired the Sitmar Line and *Fairsea* was renamed *Fair Princess*.

Above: *Island Princess* (1971/20,216 grt). (Barry Eagles)

Below: *Pacific Princess* (1971/19,903 grt). (Barry Eagles)

Spirit of London became *Sun Princess* in 1974.

Above: *Golden Princess* (1973/28,078 grt). (Barry Eagles)

Below: *Crown Princess* (1990/69,845 grt).

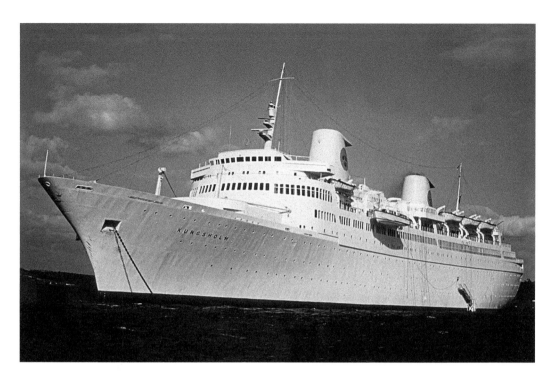

Kungsholm (1965/26,678 grt) became *Sea Princess* in 1979. (Barry Eagles)

Above: *Grand Princess* (1998/108,806 grt).

Right: *Sun Princess* (1995/77,441 grt) in the Panama Canal.

1990 *Crown Princess* advertisement.

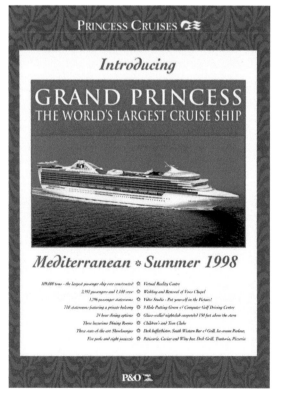

1998 'Introducing *Grand Princess* – The World's Largest Cruise Ship' advertisement.

Pacific Princess (1999/30,277 grt).

Pacific Sky sailing from Sydney on a cruise.

P&O advertisements.

Regal Princess (1991/69,845 grt).

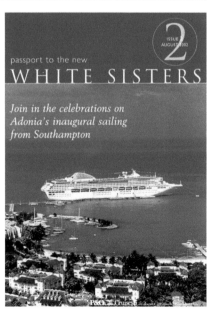

Adonia advertisement, 2002.

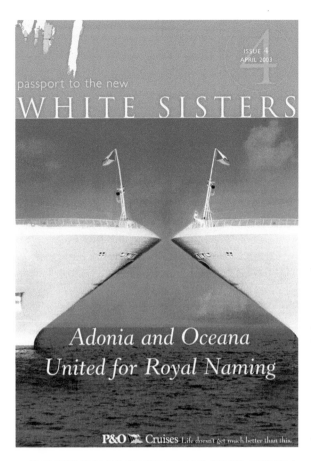

passport to the new
WHITE SISTERS

ISSUE 4
APRIL 2003

Adonia and Oceana
United for Royal Naming

P&O Cruises Life doesn't get much better than this.

Adonia (1998/77,499 grt) and *Oceana* (1999/77,499 grt) joint naming ceremony at Southampton on 21 May 2003 by HRH Princess Anne and Zara Phillips. The naming of two cruise ships simultaneously had not been seen before in Britain and marked another milestone in the history of P&O Cruises. On 24 May *Adonia* and *Oceana* made a spectacular dual sail-away from Southampton. Thousands of balloons were released from the top decks, filling the sky with the red, blue, yellow and white colours of the P&O Cruises flag. A marching band played on the quayside and a firework display ensured a dramatic departure from the Solent port. (P&O Cruises)

Oceana (2000/77,499 grt). (Barry Eagles)

P&O Spice Island Cruises, 1990/91. P&O Shipping assumed an interest in these operations and responsibility for the day-to-day management of the company. The 1990/91 cruise programme by the *Island Explorer* concentrated for ten months of the year on the islands of the Lesser Sundas from the operation's base in Bali. The island chain, stretching east from Bali to Kupang, is home to cultural enclaves that bear the mark of Hindu, Portuguese and Dutch antecedents. During the months of December and January, the ship relocated to Jakarta for a series of expedition cruises to the Krakatau volcano, Ujung Kulon Game Reserve, and South Sumatra. The 859-ton *Island Explorer* was built in 1985 and was registered in Indonesia.

P&O Premium Pacific advertisement, 2003/04.

Star Princess (1989/63,524 grt) became *Arcadia* in 1997. She was renamed *Ocean Village* in 2003 and *Pacific Pearl* in 2010.

Aurora (2000/76,152 grt) in the Panama Canal on her 2006 World Cruise.

The Penthouse Suite and the Orangery on *Aurora*.

Swan Hellenic *Minerva*
(1996/12,449 grt).

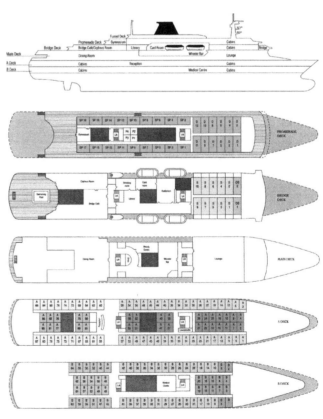

MINERVA DECK PLANS AND CABINS

Standard outside cabins on A Deck have windows, cabins on B Deck have portholes.

THE ORIANA WORLD CRUISE
X501 • 80 nights from £8,364 • 7 January to 29 March 2005

SOUTHAMPTON
Fri 7 Jan cruise check-in 2.30pm
– 4pm Sail late afternoon

PONTA DELGADA – The Azores
Mon 10 Jan arr 1.00pm
dep 6.00pm

BARBADOS
Sat 15 Jan arr 8.00am
dep midnight
EVENING IN PORT

CURACAO – Dutch Antilles
Mon 17 Jan arr 8.00am
dep 5.00pm

Transit PANAMA CANAL
Wed 19 Jan

ACAPULCO – Mexico
Sat 22 Jan arr 8.00am
dep 6.00pm

SAN FRANCISCO – USA
Wed 26 Jan arr 8.00am
dep 9.00pm

HONOLULU – Oahu,
Hawaiian Islands
Mon 31 Jan arr 8.00am
dep 6.00pm

PAGO PAGO – American Samoa
Sat 5 Feb arr 8.00am
dep 6.00pm

NUKU ALOFA – Tonga
Tue 8 Feb arr 8.00am
dep 6.00pm

AUCKLAND – New Zealand
Fri 11 Feb arr 7.00am
dep 6.00pm

SYDNEY – Australia
Mon 14 Feb arr 7.00am
dep midnight
EVENING IN PORT

BRISBANE – Australia
Wed 16 Feb arr 8.00am
dep 6.00pm

WHITSUNDAY ISLANDS –
Australia
Fri 18 Feb arr 8.00am
dep 6.00pm

KOTA KINABALU – Malaysia
Thu 24 Feb arr 8.00am
dep 6.00pm

HONG KONG
Sun 27 Feb arr 8.00am
dep 1.00am Mon 28 Feb
EVENING IN PORT

DA NANG – Vietnam
Tue 1 Mar arr 8.00am
dep 6.00pm

SINGAPORE
Fri 4 Mar arr 8.00am
dep 6.00pm

KUALA LUMPUR
(From Port Kelang) - Malaysia
Sat 5 Mar arr 8.00am
dep 6.00pm

PHUKET – Thailand
Mon 7 Mar arr 8.00am
dep 6.00pm

COLOMBO – Sri Lanka
Thu 10 Mar arr 7.00am
dep 5.00pm

COCHIN – India
Fri 11 Mar arr 9.00am
dep 6.00pm

MUMBAI – India
Sun 13 Mar arr 8.00am
dep 6.30pm

SHARM EL SHEIKH – Egypt /
Sat 19 Mar arr 7.00am
dep 6.00pm

SUEZ – Egypt
Sun 20 Mar arr 4.00am
dep 5.00am
(to disembark tour
passengers only)

Transit SUEZ CANAL
Sun 20 Mar

PORT SAID – Egypt
(to embark tour passengers)
Sun 20 Mar arr 6.00pm
dep 7.00pm

ATHENS – Greece
(from Piraeus)
Tue 22 Mar arr 8.00am
dep 6.00pm

BARCELONA – Spain
Fri 25 Mar arr 8.00am
dep 5.30pm

SOUTHAMPTON
Tue 29 Mar
arr early morning

Guide to symbols
⚓ Land by launch or tender.

Oriana (1995/69,840 grt) world cruise 2005.